The Hidden Factor

"it is," said such files
become, in time —
that be true; then
yours is one of onyx

To destroy the oyster
in eating the oyster is a great
mistake
Struck someone like the ringing of

# The Hidden Factor
## Mark and Gesture in Visual Design

Steven Skaggs

The MIT Press

Cambridge, Massachusetts

London, England

The MIT Press would like to thank the anonymous peer reviewers who provided comments on drafts of this book. The generous work of academic experts is essential for establishing the authority and quality of our publications. We acknowledge with gratitude the contributions of these otherwise uncredited readers.

This book was set in *Tome Sans Light*, a typeface designed by Delve Withrington.
Printed and bound in China.

---

Library of Congress Cataloging-in-Publication Data

Names: Skaggs, Steven, author.

Title: The hidden factor : mark and gesture in visual design / Steven Skaggs.

Description: Cambridge, Massachusetts : The MIT Press, [2023]

Identifiers: LCCN 2022059100 (print) | LCCN 2022059101 (ebook) | ISBN 9780262048569 (hardcover) | ISBN 9780262376372 (epub) | ISBN 9780262376365 (pdf)

Subjects: LCSH: Design--Human factors. | Touch.

Classification: LCC NK1520 .S58 2023 (print) | LCC NK1520 (ebook) | DDC 744--dc23/eng/20230215

LC record available at https://lccn.loc.gov/2022059100

LC ebook record available at https://lccn.loc.gov/2022059101

---

10  9  8  7  6  5  4  3  2  1

My gratitude to the artists for permission to use their work …

… with a double scoop to Laurie Doctor for allowing access

to her extraordinary daybooks and sketchbooks,

which furnish most of the illustrations that are not my own.

Preface

Artists usually think of their work as the making of an image; graphic designers think of design as communication through image and type. This book suggests that there is a third, hidden, factor at play in every visual word and image: the mark.

When they are isolated by themselves, independent of pictures or words, we notice them, but when the three ingredients are combined, marks have a funny way of disappearing from our awareness.

Of course, whether in classics such as Mendelowitz's *Drawing*, Lowenfeld's *Creative and Mental Growth*, or Arnheim's *Visual Thinking*, or in more recent works such as Tim Ingold's *Lines*, the contribution of marks to image-making has been acknowledged.

But in my view, marks deserve better. They do more than contribute to image. In this essay, the mark is elevated to share — along with image and word — the claim to being one of three equal pillars supporting all visual communication. And I want to show you how.

The key idea in this essay is this: image, word, and mark are constantly mixing; they combine in endless ways to constitute every visual message; but there is tension between them — with an especially intense tension between mark and word — that suppresses our awareness of the mark.

The narrative technique used in this book has been used before in visual culture studies, including by Marshall McLuhan, George Nelson, John Berger, April Greiman, Bruce Mau, Alan Fletcher. But we may be more familiar with it in titles such as *Goodnight Moon, Horton Hears a Who,* and *Where the Wild Things Are*; the narrative technique is that of the picture story.

By allowing the visuals to drive the narrative, I hope to make my argument self-evident and move it briskly forward. Doing that requires setting aside certain scholarly conventions; lengthy exposition, notes, even captions are avoided. Where I use someone else's term or idea, I mention them directly in the body of the text; you'll find full citations on the credits page in the back.

My hope is that the reclusive, hidden mark will begin to emerge from the shadows so we begin to see, and feel, its presence in everything around us.      — SxS

Marking, we make form to give content.

# Contents

1
From form ...

There is no visual entity without an edge.

We begin to see two edges ...

... and when we do, we begin to perceive one black line.

Those of us in the West see this line as "moving" from left to right.

In Eastern cultures, people may see this line traveling from right to left.

(But then they may have started reading this book from the other direction too!)

If we see it moving from left to right, we see it diminishing, but if we see it

moving from right to left, it seems to get thicker.

As the line gets thinner, it eventually disappears. This

place is called the "threshold of resolution." The

threshold is not a place that can be objectively

pinpointed. In each viewing situation, the

threshold will depend on a convergence of

particular conditions, such as the precision of the

reproduction process, viewing distance from the

page, level of illumination, and a viewer's eyesight.

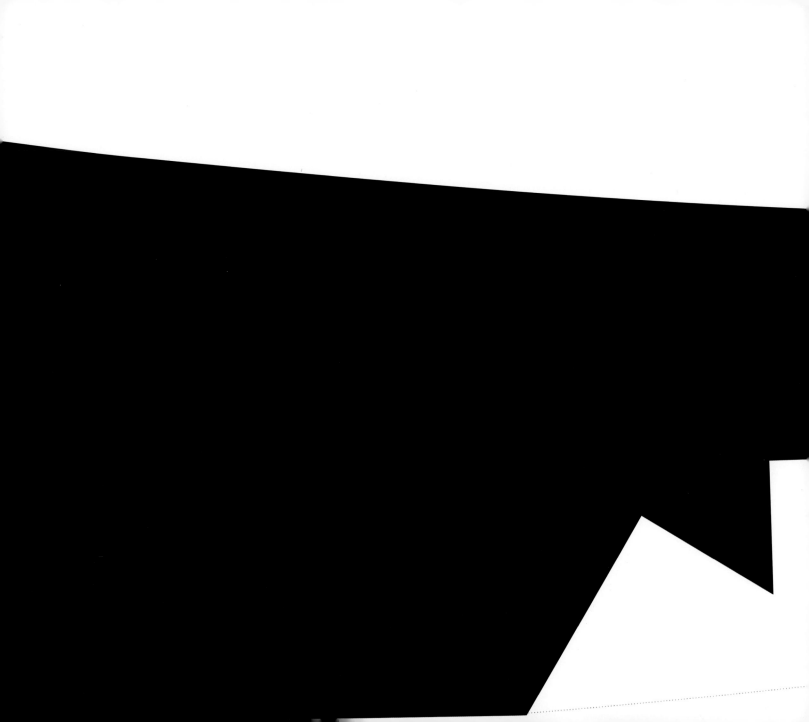

Our ability to see a line is also affected by the kind of edge it has.

If the smooth bottom edge is replaced with this jagged edge,

it becomes difficult to see it as a single black line. Now we start to see white objects

sitting atop a black surface.

When the edges of the black form are in harmony, they reinforce directionality.

Just as our ear hears two tones being "in tune," our eye senses this harmonic relationship,

and we are more likely to see the shape as a segment of a single line. We also sense a midline,

or backbone, of the directional pathway.

(The graphic devices on these pages suffer discontinuities that are unavoidable in the making of a book.

While our vision compensates for the slight bend of the paper, the breaking of continuity at the spine,

where the book's pages are bound together, is more disrupting.)

Meanwhile, although we've added just one more edge, this page looks much more complex than the

preceding page. And it remains ambiguous as we struggle to settle on a single holistic object. Is this a

white page with a black diagonal wedge above a curved black shape below? Or is it a white shape on a

black background with a little bit of white area "left over" at the top left?

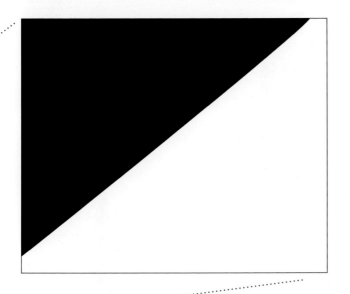

John, not known to be polite
John, known to be polite
John, known to be
John, known to me
John
J

Cropping and scaling can introduce another kind of ambiguity. Cut out a tiny portion of a gently curved shape, and the cropped edge suddenly loses its sense of curving and appears to be straight. The cropping drastically changes a visual form's character, but as long as we retain an edge, visual form itself never goes away.

So different from language, where even slight cropping (editing) may drastically change the character of what is said, while a severe level of contraction not only changes the content but eventually eradicates verbal communication itself.

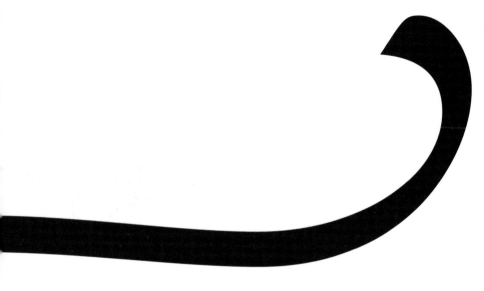

Figure/ground

Symmetry

Closure

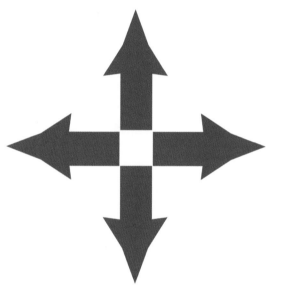

When edges conform and a line has harmony, with negative space clearly

apportioned, the resulting figure appears somehow natural and whole.

Why should it be so? It has been more than a century since such habits of

perception were identified by psychologists Max Wertheimer, Kurt Koffka,

and Wolfgang Köhler, and this is still one of the mysteries of consciousness.

Certain visual tendencies that lead to wholeness and harmony are known

as gestalt principles of perception.

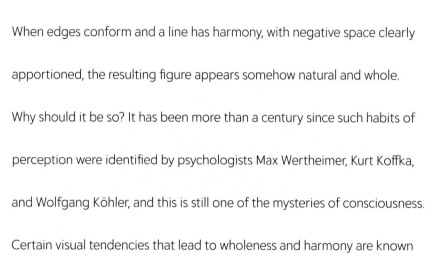

Common destination

Proximity

Similarity

Continuation

Prägnanz

This is certainly seen as

a rectangular shape.

This is just as surely seen

as a short line.

But do we see a black

rectangle containing a

white line? Black rectangle

with a gap and then a black

line? Two black rectangular

shapes?

Dynamism also plays a part, and whether something exits a frame such as a page of a book, or contains something else (like this text) within.

Ultimately, there is no clear distinction between line and shape — the terms simply serve as rough descriptions of the appearance of visual objects.

Calling something shape or line is merely a way of pointing to features of its *form*. Formalism is at the heart of the traditional "principles of art."

2
Toward content …

Formalist principles — shapes and lines, texture and shading, proportion and contrast — furnish the visual ingredients that contribute to gestalt wholeness. But when we look at something, we scarcely notice form; form perception instantly gives way to cognition, to content.

Recognizing your children in a family photograph, understanding the text when you read this book, knowing that the shop behind the striped pole is a barber's — these are all varieties of conceptual information we receive as the content of visual messages. Rarely conscious of form, we are hyper-vigilant when it comes to content. If we walked by that shop and I asked you what you saw, you would be unlikely to give a description of the form, the color and proportion of stripes on the cylinder producing a gestalt, but would simply answer "I see a barber's pole." The conceptual content of something — both direct (denotative) and associative (connotative) — is what we generally call its *meaning*.

# *Expression is* the way

We humans may not be the only ones that communicate concepts, but certainly no

other animal relies so extensively on trading complex meaning-packed symbolic

communications. We're constantly doing the work of making meaning. Perhaps it's

because we have evolved to be such über-communicators of conceptual content that

we remain so oblivious to the *expression* of the form.

form

In broadest terms, expression is the way form makes us feel. A square is not only

mathematically or intellectually different from a circle — it feels different from a circle.

A line drawn with a straight edge projects a different emotional feeling than one

dragged by an ink-laden brush. How these feelings are generated from visual form

alone — completely apart from the emotions that ensue from the content — is another

*makes us feel*

great mystery in the philosophy of mind. But a part of that power of expression comes

from our sense of how the form was made, what brought it into the world.

Understanding expression starts with understanding marks. Marking is the beginning point in the process of making anything visual — from the ceiling of the Sistine Chapel to disposable packaging we toss aside everyday in our consumerist culture. Marking is the source of all manifest form, the expression-spring from which flow all of our sensibilities that are outside the content itself. If we reserve the word "meaning" for only the conceptual content of something, then expression is all the feeling-effects around how something looks, how something is made, how something comes to be the way it is. To best study what marking is we have to drill down to the passionate center — to that most expressive kind of visual thing — the raw, gestured mark. The purpose of this essay is to investigate it in depth. To get there, we have to start by taking a look at the larger realm of marking as a whole.

# 3
## ...Through marking

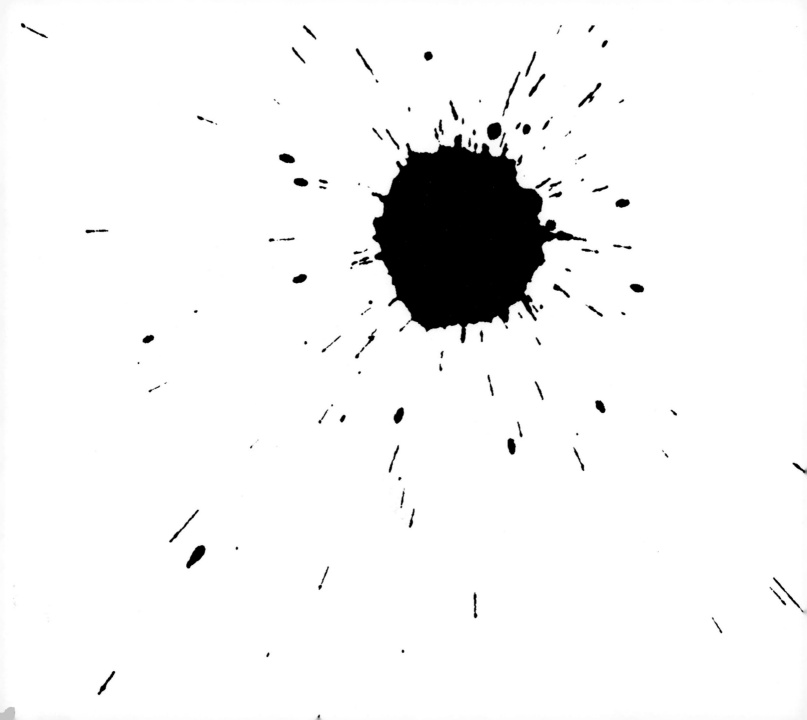

Marking is a physical interaction between things that leaves behind a visible trace. It's possible to make a mark

with radiant energy (sunburn) or organic processes (mold), but usually a mark is caused by the contact of two

physical surfaces rubbing against each other: a tire skid on pavement, a tree branch scraping the side of a house, ink

brushed onto paper, the impression of type letterpressed into the fibers of handmade paper.

Something subtle but important happens when we see a mark. Pay attention to form and we notice its features

as shape and line; consider content and we refer to its conceptual meaning; but marks always allude to a past

action: the event that caused the mark to become. Every time we see a mark, we supply an interpretation of what

happened to leave such a trace. A mark is evidence of its own making.

CONCEPTUAL CONTENT

MEANING IMPULSE

MARKING

How can something so central to visual life be so forgotten? The

drive toward conceptual content — the "meaning impulse" — is so

great that we become less aware of the coming-into-being that

is the mark. The meaning impulse suppresses our awareness of

marking. Yet the mark continues to exert its effect even when we

think we are not noticing it. We continue to supply interpretations

about what made it, who made it, and when it may have been made.

The evidence of contact is also evidence of motion — and emotion.

Whether geometric and static or rapidly dashed out, touched light

as a kiss or stabbed violently, marks are the fundamental source of

expression, giving feeling to form.

When spontaneously and gesturally made, the markedness of a

visual thing is obvious, but many times the marking has evolved

into visual forms that are less clearly the result of movement.

There are examples all around us of this "fossilized" movement,

and we will look at some instances of them as we dig deeper into

the kinds of marks and how marks work on us.

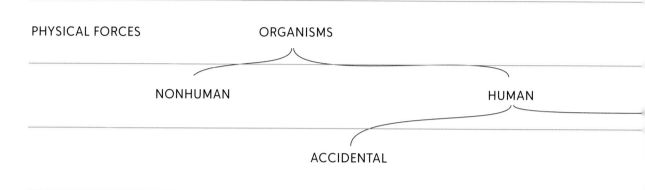

PHYSICAL FORCES          ORGANISMS

NONHUMAN                              HUMAN

ACCIDENTAL

There are many different kinds of marks, some made by natural forces such as you might

find in a splatter of paint, others representing intentional traces made by people in various

communicative arts. The branching diagram on this and the following pages shows some of the

most important varieties. The next several pages focus on just a portion of these marks: the

ones people intentionally make.

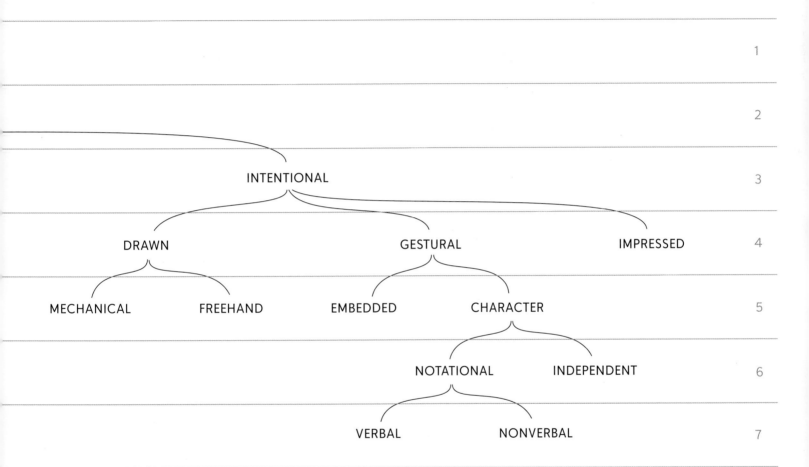

When we see marks that people have made, we see them either as accidental by-

products of doing something else — like footprints or paint drips — or as intentional

attempts to signal, express, communicate. Intentional marks imply a purpose of

some kind, an effort to *represent*, to deliver something from our inner world to the

outer, public world.

Intentional marks fall into three general families: drawn, gestural, and impressed. Whether

or not they portray an external subject, what is essential to drawings is that they are

built up, constructed over time, usually a composite of other marks. Gestural marks

emphasize the momentary movement of a body, usually in an instant. Impressed marks,

such as stamping, imprinting, gouging, and cutting, emphasize pressure: squeezing,

deflecting, and deforming a material rather than a sweep across a material's surface.

# INTENTIONAL HUMAN-MADE MARKS

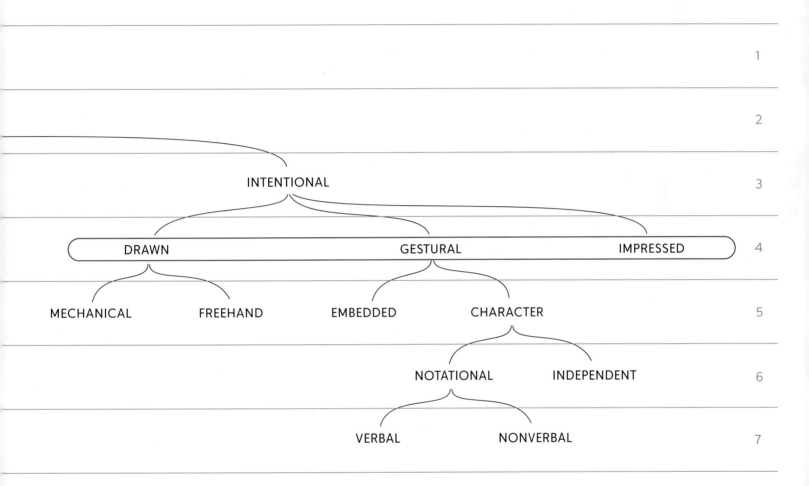

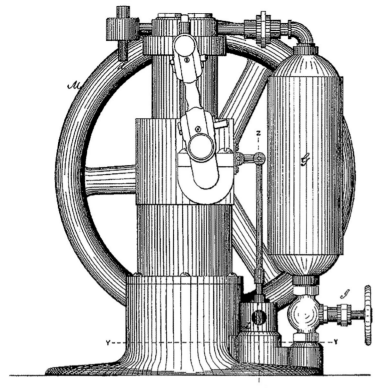

Mechanical drawings aim for geometric precision and use prepared instruments to assist in the process. Traditional mechanical drawing tools such as compass, triangle, and T-square have been replaced by digital Bézier curves and equipment that is virtual. Today's mechanical drawing is distinguished solely by the resulting accuracy of its geometrical coordinates.

Freehand drawings lack the geometric precision of a mechanical drawing; yet, like most mechanical drawings and unlike purely gestural markings, freehand drawings usually reference a subject — a "likeness" beyond the body's movement.

# INTENTIONAL HUMAN-MADE MARKS

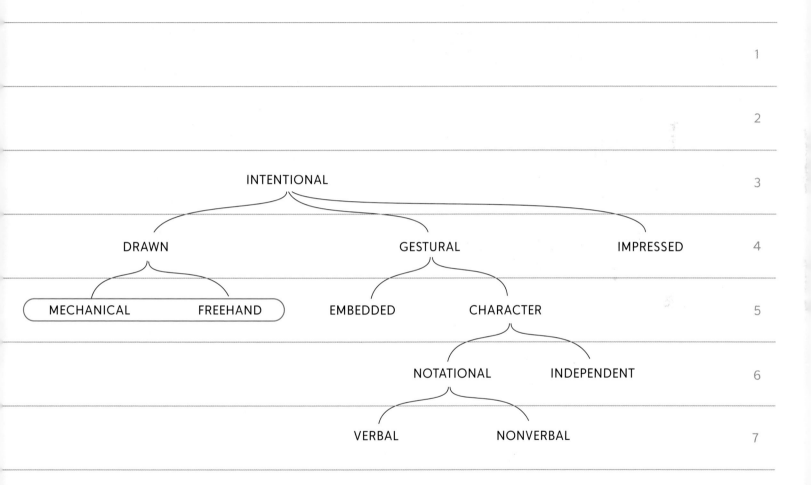

INTENTIONAL

DRAWN  GESTURAL  IMPRESSED

MECHANICAL  FREEHAND  EMBEDDED  CHARACTER

NOTATIONAL  INDEPENDENT

VERBAL  NONVERBAL

1

2

3

4

5

6

7

Like all gestural marks, embedded gestural marks suggest

the movement of the body. But unlike character marks,

embedded gestural marks are seen as part of a larger

freehand drawing, such as marks made to build up a

texture, or to depict a surface. Whether long scribblings

or massed cross hatchings, what characterizes them is

that we simply see them as part of some greater whole.

Character marks are gestural marks that have a sense

of their own clear identity as visual objects. The gesture

itself is emphasized, with its clear sequence of strokes

and movements. While an isolated single element

of an embedded gesture may look like a character

mark, character marks always retain their own discrete

individuality, a trait that is lacking in the stipplings,

shadings, cross hatchings of embedded gestures.

# INTENTIONAL HUMAN-MADE MARKS

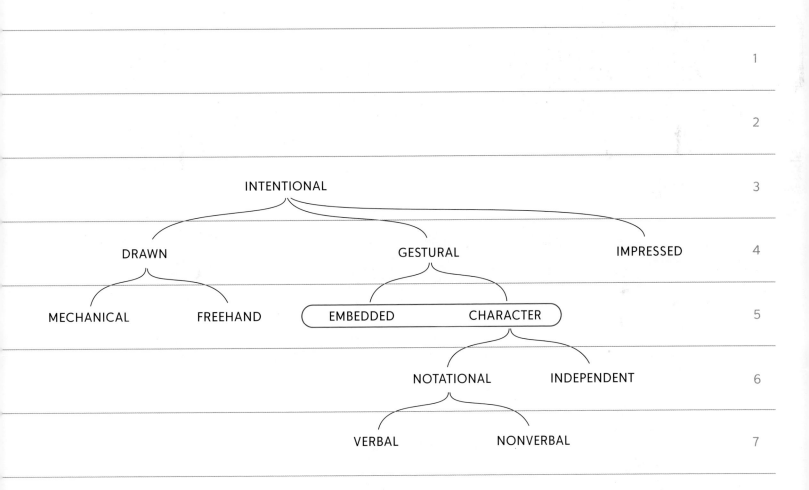

Character marks have another very important attribute: they are the kind of graphic element at the foundation of almost all written languages. Even so, there remain many independent character marks that are not a part of any written language or other notational code system.

A notational code is a set of assigned meanings attached to visual signs or strings of visual signs, so that when the signs are used according to certain rules, conceptual information may be communicated.

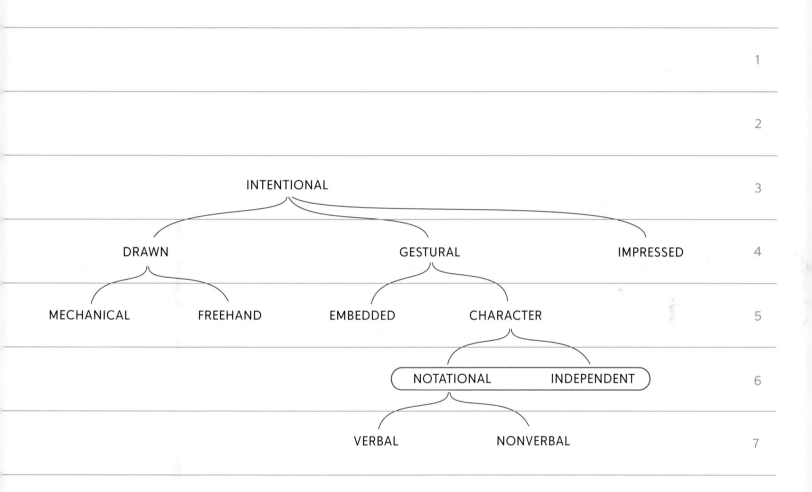

INTENTIONAL HUMAN-MADE MARKS

INTENTIONAL

DRAWN        GESTURAL        IMPRESSED

MECHANICAL        FREEHAND        EMBEDDED        CHARACTER

NOTATIONAL        INDEPENDENT

VERBAL        NONVERBAL

1
2
3
4
5
6
7

45

Some notational codes are verbal (like typography) and others are nonverbal (such as electrical schematics). The notational code system you are reading now is called the alphabet. A particular stylistic genre of a notational code is called a script. For example, within the notational code of the alphabet, blackletter is a script, as are roman, italic, and cursive (with subvariants within those classes).

Written languages are the most common type of coded notational systems, but nonverbal notational systems surround us as well. Examples include the symbol sets found in technical instructions, such as medical and astronomical signs, or the musical notes written in a score. Even choreographers and aerobatic pilots use notational code systems.

ABCDEF
GHIJKL
MNOPR
STUVW
XYZ

INTENTIONAL HUMAN-MADE MARKS

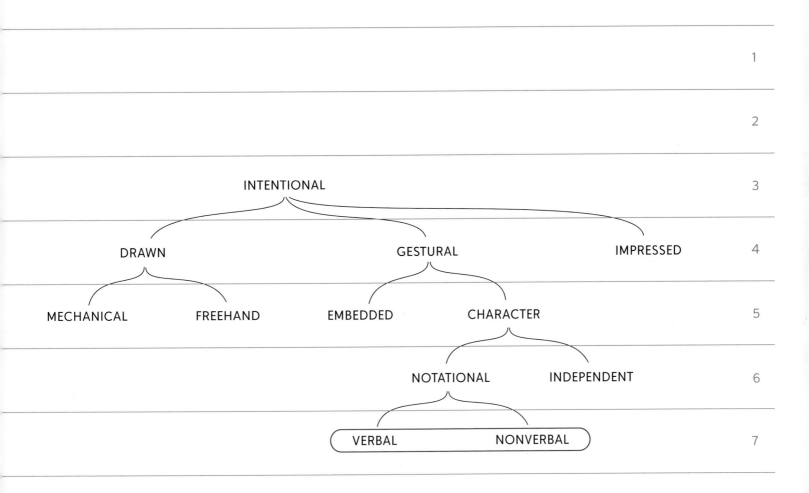

By the way, linguists call the visual characters of a notational code "graphemes," and they call the various alternate forms of graphemes "allographs." For our purpose, we will use terms that better reflect historical usage from our visual point of view. All the characters illustrated here are the letter Q (in the alphabet notational code), and despite their different appearances, all but two belong to the roman script. The other two? One is blackletter and one is an archaic form known as a Lombardic initial. Typographers next divide letter forms into subcategories called families. Five of the Qs here fall into a family known as sans serif, and the others belong to the serif family (even though none of those here exhibit even the hint of a serif!). It goes to show how slippery and difficult it is to pin down visual signs, which always present new variants that challenge the best attempts to classify and name.

*Lombardic
°Blackletter

It's unfortunate that, in the English language, our word "writing" is so ambiguous. Sometimes it's used to refer to the authoring of text, as when we say "Hemingway was a fine writer." But at other times it refers to the notational code that conveys any author's text, as when we say "Writing first developed in Mesopotamia." Yet again, we might hear "Mary is an excellent writer but her writing is illegible." The prefix "hand-" is often inserted to help clarify things: "handwriting." Only in this last sense do we emphasize the making of marks. But then what do we call "written" marks that are not notational, or marks that, while notational, are yet not fully verbal?

Since our interest here is visual, we will use the word "writing" to refer to graphic writing in all its many manifestations. In this graphic sense, we should take writing in the broadest way possible: writing (as a verb) is the action of making character marks; writing (as a noun) refers to the graphic character marks that have been made. We can use the term whether the characters belong to a notational code system (linguistic or nonlinguistic) or are independent of any system. Considered as visual gesture, writing is relieved from the weight of linguistics, from questions of literacy or fluency; writing is shielded from the pressure to be readable. For the writer, at least from a graphical perspective, legibility is a choice.

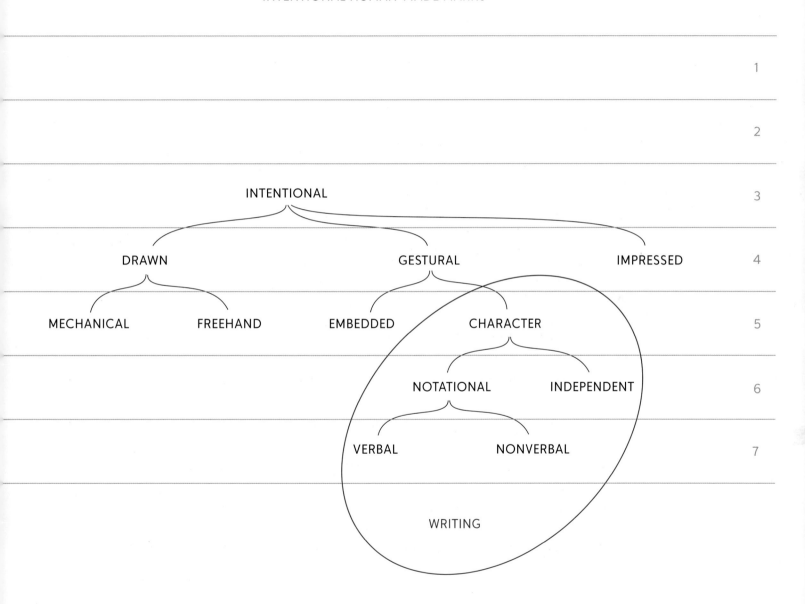

INTENTIONAL HUMAN-MADE MARKS

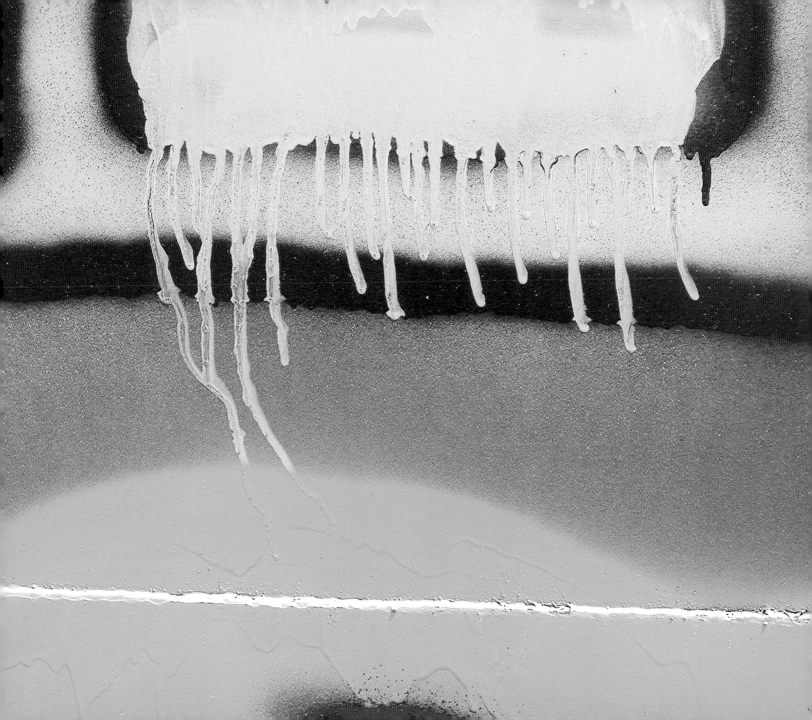

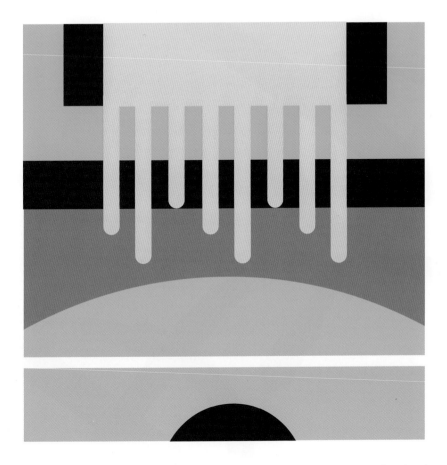

A transformation is when one kind of mark is translated into another kind.

Every kind of mark can be transformed. The transformation changes the evidence of the original mark, often rationalizing proportions and sharpness of lines. When we speak of fossilized gestures, we refer to gestural marks that have gone through this kind of transformative process.

For instance, a freely written character can be adapted into a mechanically drawn glyph through a process called stylization. Stylization distills the form to essentials. The original freely written character mark on the far left might be moderately stylized by editing out accidental details of the brush while retaining the essential gestural flow, or we might go farther, seeking to find in the character its purest geometric shapes, such as the version on this page. Stylization is especially relevant in the design of logos and in font design, where the glyphs are intended to be used in many sizes and perceptual conditions.

The Arabic character siin in the typefaces Adobe *Naskh* (left) and *Myriad Arabic* (right) reflect different stylization decisions. Muhammad Zuhair Ruhani Bazi's typeface *Naskh* is based closely on the calligraphic character in an Ottoman manuscript. It is a written form, then stylized to highlight smoothness.

Robert Slimbach's *Myriad Arabic* retains some of the flow of the original gesture, but the treatment of terminals and transitional movements is nothing like what would happen in writing. They have been adapted to fit the more mechanical, industrial style of *Myriad*, the font family of which *Myriad Arabic* is a part.

We see these decisions in Western typography too. Despite several stages of stylization, Linotype *Palatino Italic* (1948) still reveals its gestural, calligraphic roots. The characters began as designer Hermann Zapf's calligraphic pen-made character marks, which Zapf then revised freehand with black and white inks. Technicians at Stempel type foundry provided further drawings, making the necessary adjustments to render the forms as a metal font. Then, in the 1990s, Linotype artists digitally mapped and edited the font further for production in desktop publishing. Yet gestures remain:

1 — The opening move is not a true serif but an entry stroke used to encourage ink to begin flowing from the chisel-cut pen. It also allows the connecting of one character to the next in cursive handwriting.

2 — The bottom of the downstroke flares slightly, a trait known as "entasis," reflecting the effect of increasing pen pressure at a stroke's beginning and conclusion. The lopped-off point is a vestigial element from when the typeface was originally cast in metal (acute points would wear down quickly in metal).

3 — The branching structure's thin line reflects the upward gesture of the pen made with light pressure.

4 — The transition back to a thick stroke happens naturally when a chisel-point pen changes direction.

5 — The character terminates with a sense of increased pressure and an exit stroke at 40 degrees: the angle that produces the thinnest line from a chisel-cut pen.

*Arno* (Robert Slimbach, 2007) is a Venetian Old Style typeface that retains the feel of the nib through its translation to digital technologies. The gestures within the parts are retained.

The influence of the handmade mark (as opposed to the mechanically drawn geometrical shape) extends even to the dot of the i, where the irregularity is dynamically balanced within a perfect circle it only suggests.

Compare it to the decisions made in the drafting of *Bodoni 72* (Dmitry Kirsanov, 1994), where the distillation of the dot departs from geometric perfection only to account for the influence of optical illusion.

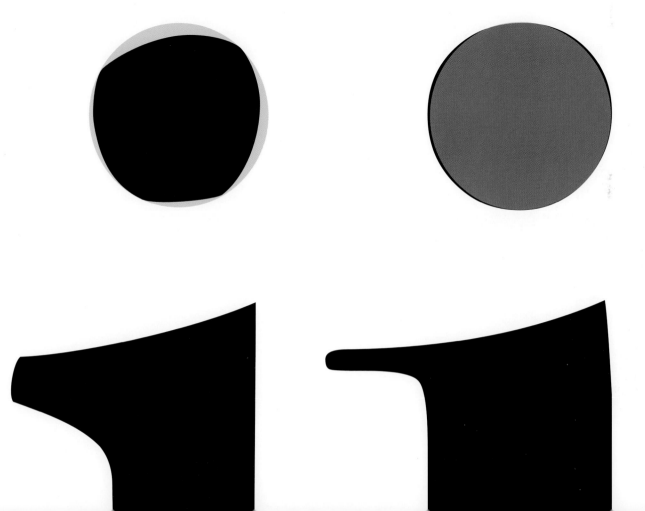

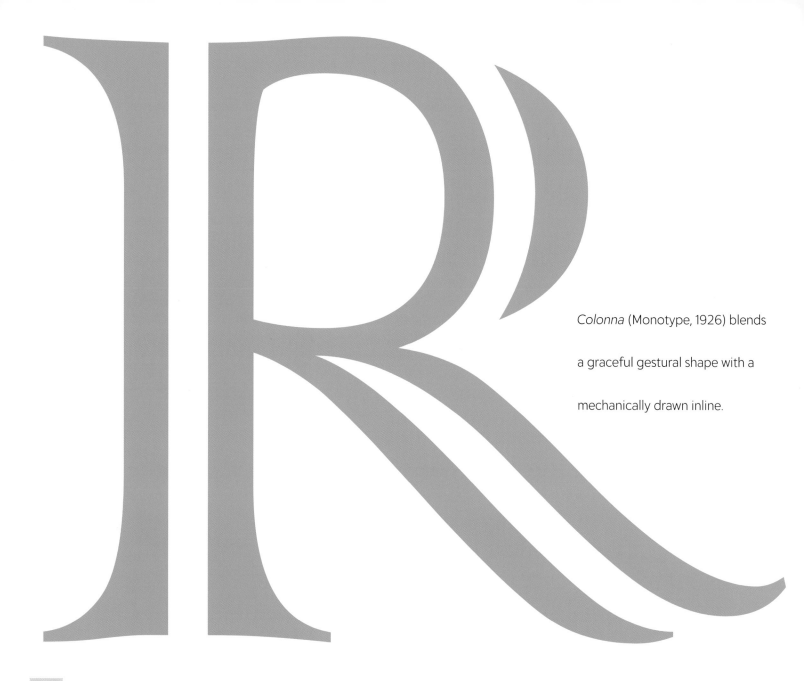

*Colonna* (Monotype, 1926) blends

a graceful gestural shape with a

mechanically drawn inline.

The typeface *Blasphemy* (Delve Withrington, 2010) features a set of digital tablet gestures which contradict the fundamental form of the character. But — voilà! — the perceptual gestalt magically restores the conventional form.

This dance between gestural mark and stylized drawings can be seen by looking at even the most conventional typefaces through history, as shown next …

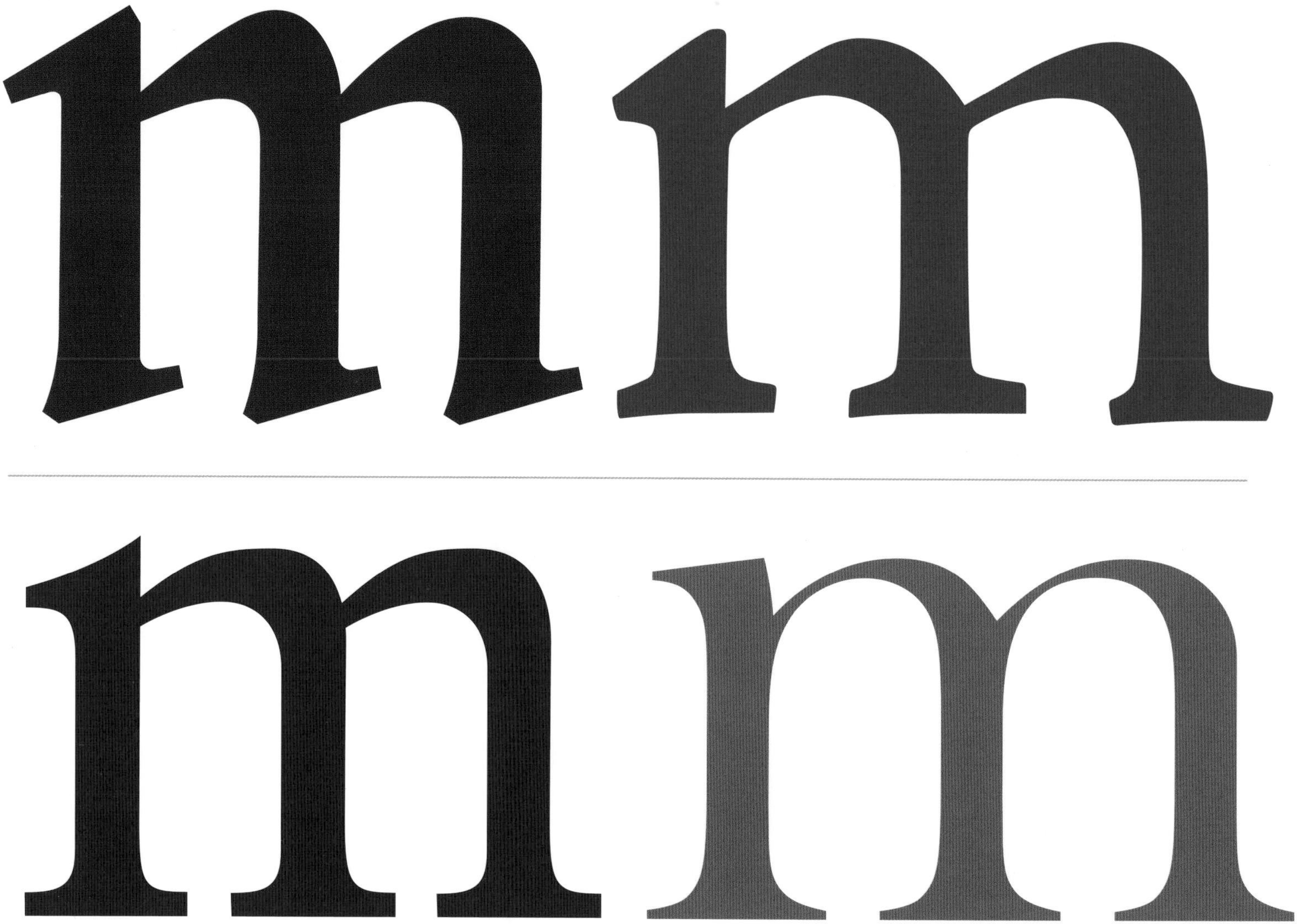

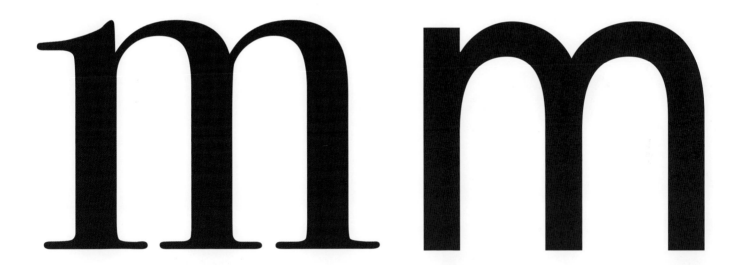

- Early roman types retained gestures of the scribes' pen such as exit strokes (Sweynheym and Pannartz, 1465).

- Nicolas Jenson decisively moved from the pen to better adapt to the technology of metal (1470).

- By the seventeenth century the forms had evolved to be more regular and uniform (Christoffel van Dijck, 1650).

- Hot-press paper allowed for finer thins and continued "rationalization" (John Baskerville, 1757).

- Extreme rational precision was suggested by "modern" typefaces (Giambattista Bodoni, 1795).

- Departure from the hand was seemingly complete by early twentieth-century sans serifs (*Futura*, Paul Renner, 1927).

Even in most sans serif typefaces, such as *Helvetica* (Max Miedinger, 1957), vestigial influences of writing peek from beneath the rationalized drawings of their forms. The strokes of *Helvetica* appear at first glance to be uniform, but they subtly change weight. Some of the fluctuation in weight is to correct for optical illusions. For instance, verticals are a bit heavier than horizontals to suggest the sturdiness necessary to act as "supports." Strokes attenuate where they converge, such as when the branching region of the n becomes thinner as it encounters the vertical. This counters the tendency for the eye to see junctions as heavier weight.

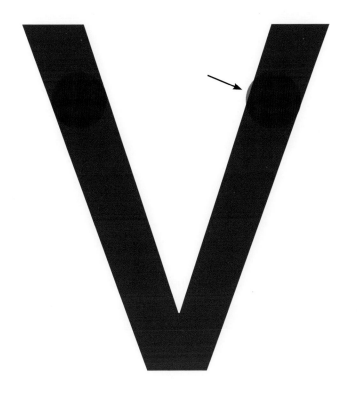

But a different kind of optical correction appears on the right-hand stroke of the v, w, and y. There is no clear perceptual or form-based reason why the right-hand stroke should need to be lightened in order to appear correct — except the visual habituation of seeing characters made by handwriting. The right stroke of a v is the upstroke of a letter handwritten with a pointed pen, a stroke made with less pressure, and therefore thinner. Based on the nineteenth-century *Akzidenz Grotesque, Helvetica* probably shows the effects of longstanding accommodation to the effects of written gestures.

These examples demonstrate that marking covers an enormous

territory: illegible graphic marks that act as location markers or may

reflect a capricious moment's expression; writing in which gestures

are constrained to begin to reveal a notational code; carefully

drawn typographic characters in which gestural qualities are nearly

eliminated in order to push forward the conventional forms of letters

and make a text instantly readable.

Next, we will look at a model that allows us to see the entire scope of

the landscape of imagery, words, and marking and how they interact

so that forms develop both expression and conceptual content. And

we will see how tension arises between the meaning impulse and the

sense of gestural freedom.

# 4
# The visual gamut

Pictographic

Alphabetic

Independent

Imagine three freely written character marks. One resembles an object, say a fish. The second suggests a letter

of the alphabet. The third is an independent gestural expression. These three samples point toward a branching

structure in which marks divide along three distinct modes by which visual information is conveyed. The

pictographic character strives to communicate through image. The alphabetic character wants to communicate

through use of words. Meanwhile the independent nameless gestural form retains its presence as pure mark.

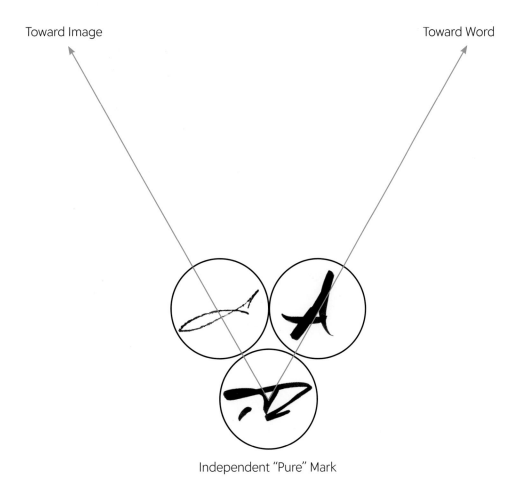

Toward Image

Toward Word

Independent "Pure" Mark

From this foundational branching idea, we can imagine the range of visual entities as they climb up, away from pure abstract markings, and diverge to become increasingly focused on the role of image or of word.

The perfect likeness

The most legible

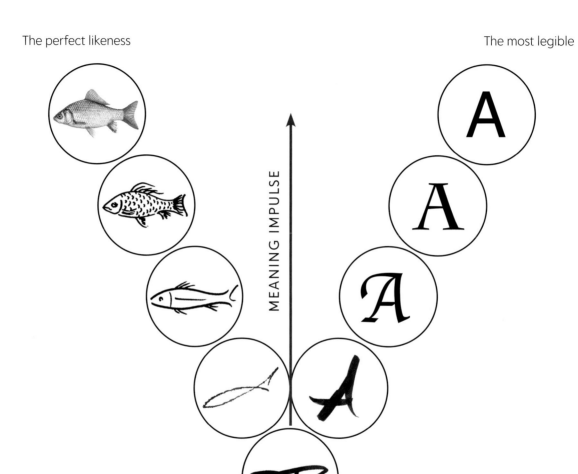

MEANING IMPULSE

The purely gestural

We can think of these ranges as being comprised of as many steps as we like; here we show a five-step sequence. At the top are extremes reserved for the most perfect likeness of a subject on one side, and the most legible possible typography on the other. The meaning impulse drives us to want to see conceptual clarity in word and image. Moving downward, the two ranges converge toward the purely gestural mark. They converge because as they lose likeness and legibility — the traits that give them semantic clarity — they are left with the only thing that marks inherently do: give evidence of their own production as traces of kinetic material contact. Conversely, as the ranges move upward toward image or toward word, they diverge due to how differently representational images and graphic words function as signs. Image and word are two very different ways of conveying conceptual information; only language can fully communicate conceptual propositions and claims about the world, while only an image can visually stand in as a surrogate, a simulacrum, posing as a visual slice of that world. Marking, meanwhile, always talks of history, of an action that once happened but is no more.

By extending this idea we can construct the gamut of possible modes of visual reference. The visual gamut reveals the full playground — the semantic plane — upon which visual entities interact. The labels on the diagram use the terms mark, word, and image. These are shorthands; so to better define them:

**Image** = That which represents a subject through likeness, resemblance, iconicity.

**Word** = That which communicates through symbol systems, especially linguistic and other notational codes.

**Mark** = Indexically recorded evidence of movement, material contact, especially human gesture.

We've often heard graphic design described as communication through word and image. But instead of a simple binary choice between word and image, we discover we have a larger and more nuanced semantic surface of complex graphic interaction. In addition to the factors of image and word, there is the third, hidden factor: marks. When we include marks as an indispensable player, the trivalent gamut suddenly brims with possibilities. Let's investigate what this diagram can tell us …

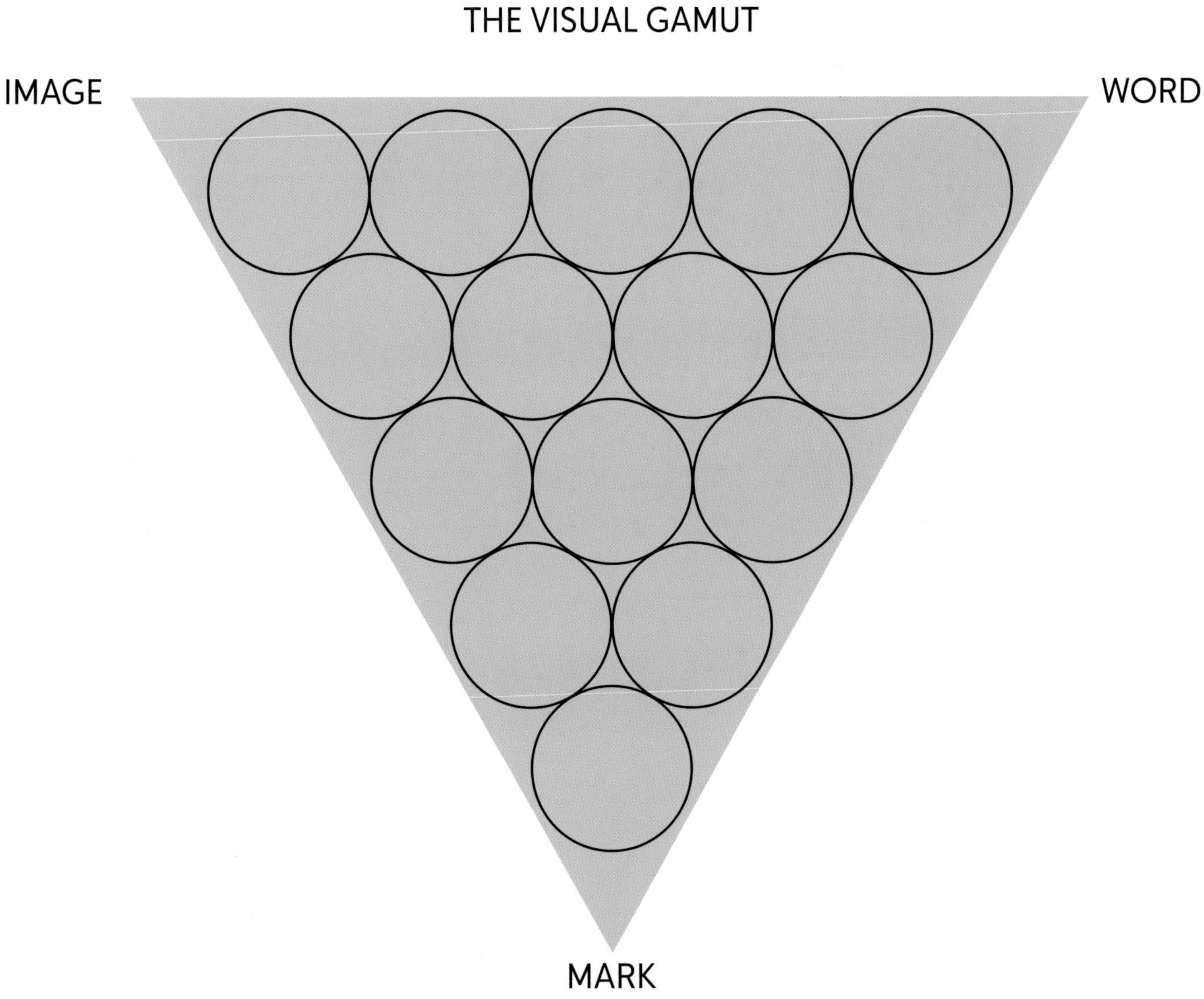

THE VISUAL GAMUT

IMAGE

WORD

MARK

IMAGE    WORD

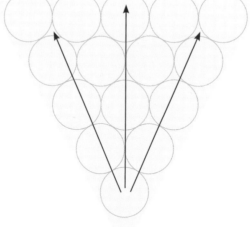

MARK

As we move from the region of pure mark upward, we lose a sense of the gesture, the haptic, the world of movement and touch; these are sacrificed in order to gain conceptual clarity in language or in representational image. Indeed, for the sake of conceptual clarity, they *must* be sacrificed. When the focus of attention is on the making of the sign, we make no assertion about the world. The pure mark simply is in the world and of the world. So while a graffitist's tag might be said to make a claim of subversive identity, it's actually the transgression itself and the logo-esque aspects of the tag that are doing the talking. The mark — as mark, per se — simply reveals the pure expressive sensation in and of its own making.

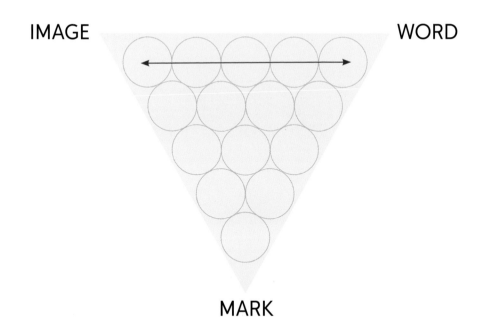

IMAGE          WORD

MARK

Image portrays; it claims to document, in precise detail, its subject in a moment in time. In doing so, image reveals.

Language permits us not only to reveal, but to make assertions about the world. Consequently, both image and word

are distant from the pure expression of the making that we find in the gestural mark. Their graphic modes intend a

conceptual side marks lack. Keep in mind that in the gamut, "word" indicates typography and other notational codes.

Word is not about the story in the book, but the typography that enables it; not the music as heard, but the printed score

that is read for its performance. This is the region of show and tell: images show us, words tell us, about the world.

IMAGE                      WORD

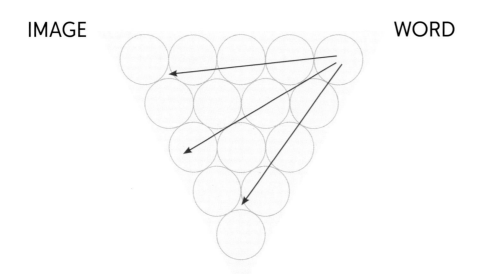

MARK

The word corner of the gamut stands for typography and other notational codes that are symbol systems. Language

is the "big boss." The dominance of language is so great that when we see a sentence printed in a legible font, we are

hardly even aware that we are *seeing* anything at all. When we read we are blind. In the visual gamut, the farther we move

from the word apex, the more we regain sight. The visual becomes more available, the big boss releases complete control

over our eyes. The ability to clearly articulate propositional ideas through language begins to weaken. What do we gain?

Sensuality: representation of the world (image) and the traces left by bodies moving through it (mark).

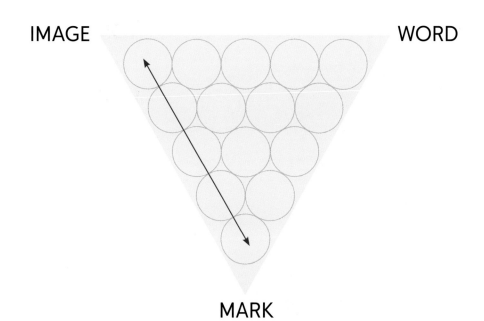

IMAGE          WORD

MARK

Image and mark are unable to convey the coded linguistic complexities made possible by the visual glyphs of a font, but still there is a spectrum of possibilities between them. The further we move from image to mark, the more we introduce liveliness and activity of line, and with it a sense of the personal, the artist, a maker working in a certain material medium at a particular instant of time. Moving from mark to image we leave the acted-upon and emphasize the gazed-upon world of the represented subject. In a sense, we move from verb to noun, from the nameless to the named.

IMAGE 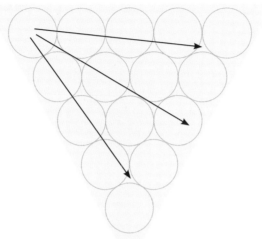 WORD

MARK

By leaving image behind, we leave the direct model to our eyes, the simulacrum of the representational figure. We exchange the apparitional or phenomenal, the implied (although possibly conjured) documentation of a scene — the visual proposition of "what is" — and we move toward the ephemeral collision of materials (mark) or the conceptual authority of logic and language (word).

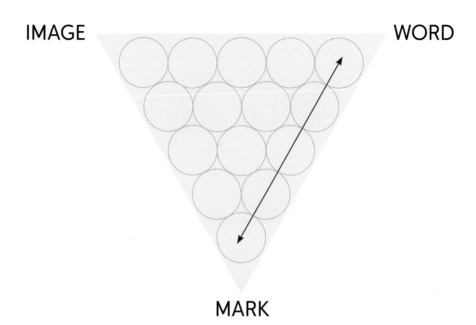

IMAGE        WORD

MARK

The spectrum between mark and word departs from the visual documentation of subjects as they appear in the world.

Marks supply kinetics. Marks are haptic, body-forward records, evidence of contact between objects in the world. Words

of a text convey an author's intricate conceptual thoughts. Although a text may describe the visual appearance of an

image or a mark, it can do this only through the letter forms that are themselves neutral, arbitrary to the story they tell.

Legible text typography is comprised of the most selfless of graphic symbols — without special training in art and design

school, we generally are only aware of the verbal information we receive through them.

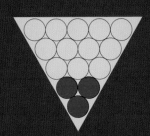

# 5
# Material forward: the clear mark

Marks are about materiality. The body, the paint, the

motion of contact. Lacking a sense of intentionality,

the marks shown here will not likely be seen as

human-made gestures. Yet artists frequently make

use of jabbing, scraping, and other mechanical

processes such as these to provide textural depth

that provides expression within a larger work of art.

A sense of intention can be supplied by information

outside the marking, such as by the use of mats,

frames, and gallery walls. But absent such cues,

marks such as these would likely go unnoticed as a

form of human communication.

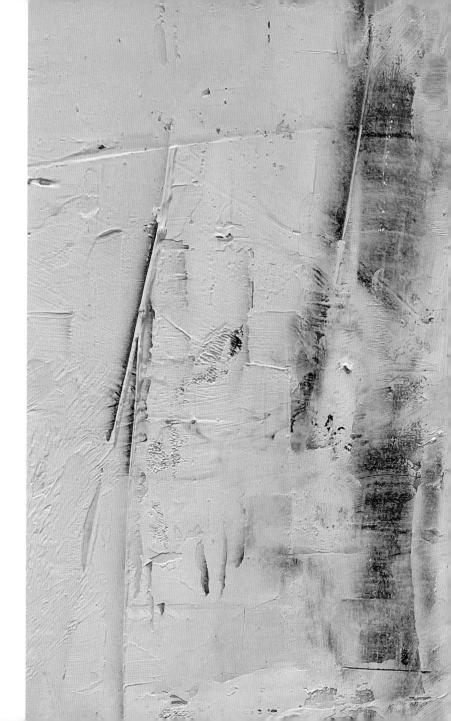

But these marks, simple as they are, project an unmistakable sense of human intention. The subtle bowing of the line segments, their approximate equality in length, the evenness of the texture they produce, the sense of pressure distribution along the length of each are all evidence that we feel immediately in our body. These are not simply random marks; they are strokes. Dutch typographer Gerrit Noordzij considered the stroke to be the foundation of both writing and typography: "A stroke is the uninterrupted trace of an implement on the writing plane." But what exactly constitutes a stroke is a difficult question. Is it any gestured movement on a surface? A movement in one direction until it changes course? Is it the entire period between pen contact and pen lift? A stroke is a mark made with intention, from the moment of initiation until a significant pause. After the pause, the stroke ends. Here the tool may be lifted, or a new impulse can begin in another direction. A stroke is like a breath. It is a pulse with a beginning, a sense of inevitable flow, and then it ends in a lift, or some clear other pulse.

Strokes are gestured moments: drawings are built up with time. Sometimes a series of strokes occupy

the space between pure gesture and careful drawing. When we attempt to make geometric figures or

diagrams, our mind's intent and the strictures of geometry constrain our hands. Yet, with practice, an

artist can "gesture-draw" geometric forms with speed and a great degree of freedom of movement.

Appearing neither uncertain nor coldly mathematical, such figures can possess great energy and

expression. Most of us would say the drawing on the right is made up of four black strokes and some

larger number of yellow ones, "coloring in" the interior of the square.

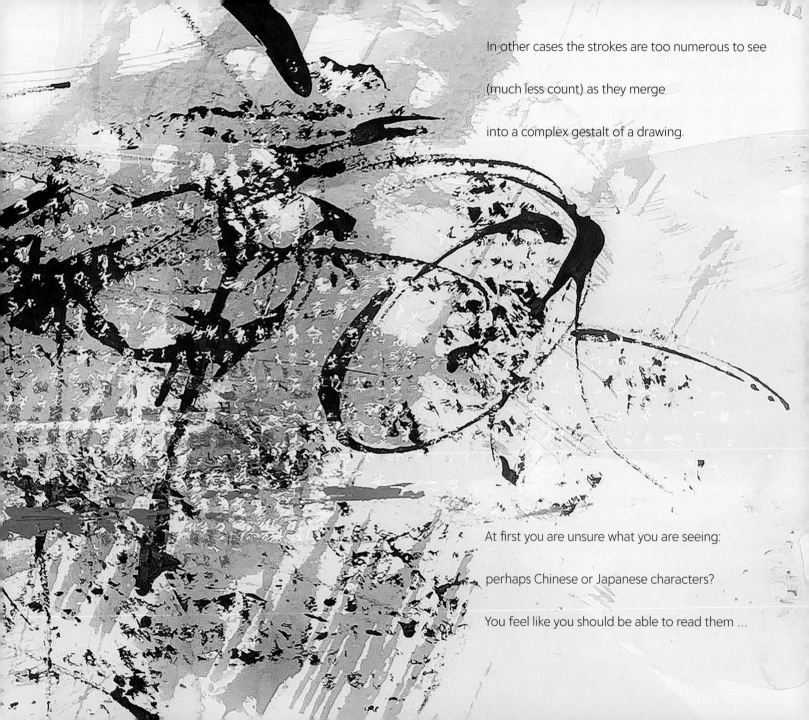

In other cases the strokes are too numerous to see

(much less count) as they merge

into a complex gestalt of a drawing.

At first you are unsure what you are seeing:

perhaps Chinese or Japanese characters?

You feel like you should be able to read them ...

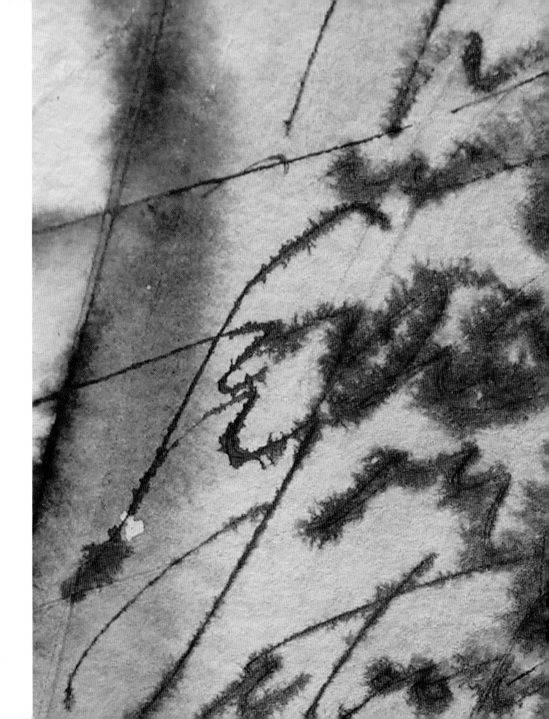

... or the "strokiness" begins to

melt away entirely though you

feel sure there must be language

in those gestural movements of

nib, brush, or chalk, even if it is not

a language you understand. Such

liminal examples place you on the

borderline between two worlds,

language and expressive marking,

marking and wording. In the end,

the important thing is not the

stroke but the effect of the whole,

as played out on the semantic

plane of the visual gamut.

Marking predominates here, but,

should the marks suddenly be

recognized as alphabet, we immediately

gain a strong connotation of language,

even in the absence of actual text.

Even if you know Latin, the unusual form of this writing would take some effort to read, as it foregrounds the text's visual form at the expense of its verbal content. The effort might seem frustrating, slowing you up. Or we may simply enjoy the visual game. We sense words even if we can't read Latin, and we feel a bit of tension in our desire to know what it says.

Somehow we don't feel the same tension when the marks occupy the borderline

between expressive mark-making and a visual representation. Why is it that we are

more comfortable at the image/mark border than we are at the word/mark border?

A question we'll return to.

6

Concept forward: the clear image

The conceptually clear image relies on resemblance, iconicity.

The conceptually clear image looks *like* something: its subject.

Mark-making gives way to representation.

With photography, the transformation is so complete that we often forget that

light performs a kind of mark-making of its own, reflecting from the subject to

a photoreceptor cell in the camera (or in the eye).

The verisimilitude of proportion

and texture gradient

and other visual cues

encourages us to accept

the image as the thing itself.

Most representational

images reveal their subjects

through careful likenesses,

yet it is possible for images

to remain clear through

considerable simplification …

... Sometimes the simplification can be extreme, as in this petroglyph

scratched into a rock by indigenous people in the New Mexican desert.

A knife scraping stone limits the amount of detail, but if the intent

is to depict the concept "Thunderbird" — a form that is habituated —

then more detail is not needed. As the drawing's technique hides the

individual gestures of the tool, the designer sacrifices self-expression

in favor of rendering a conceptual and symbolic figure. Such simplified

picures are called pictographs.

Even as we appreciate the

artistry, we are compelled

toward the subject matter.

Our attention turns from the

marking and making and we

feel conceptual questions

arise: What are the soldiers

doing? Who is this strange

and wonderful giant man?

Indications of the meaning

impulse at work.

rst place, to recapitulate, as clearly as possible, what our
with respect to the fundamental nature of our sensuous
general. We have intended, then, to say that all our intuition
othing but the representation of phenomena; that the things
e intuite, are not in themselves the same as our representation
em in intuition, nor are their relations in themselves so con
s they appear to us; and that if we take away the subject, or
nly the subjective constitution of our senses in general, then
nly the nature and relations of objects in space and time, but
pace and time themselves disappear; and that these, as phenom
annot exist in themselves, but only in us. What may be the
f objects considered as things in themselves and without refer
the receptivity of our sensibility is quite unknown to us. We
othing more than our mode of perceiving them, which is pe
s, and which, though not of necessity pertaining to every

# 7

# Concept forward: the clear word

Mine eyes h

*Baskerville*, John Baskerville (1757)

Mine eyes have s

*Helvetica Neue*, Max Miedinger (1957, 1983)

e eyes have seer

*Century Schoolbook*, Morris Fuller Benton (1919)

ne eyes have seen

Mine eyes have s

ne eyes have see

*Palatino*, Hermann Zapf (1949)

the glory of the

When we move up the right side of the gamut away from the gestural mark toward the region of conceptual clarity, we pass a magic threshold. At some point, we go from seeing graphic signs as marks to understanding them as words. It's the sudden and harsh cognitive transformation called "reading." Our experience of expressive form is catapulted into voices, and the conceptual world of language flashes open. In this new land, the haptic is forgotten and the word rules.

*Galliard,* Matthew Carter (1978)

*Optima,* Hermann Zapf (1958)

*Tome,* Delve Withrington (2017)

Typefaces that are designed for easy reading are carefully drafted with geometric details

that serve to minimize, stylize, and rationalize the original gesture. Such typefaces appear

more permanent, neutral, objective — sacrificing the whim of individuality in order to

speak more from a distance, less emotionally — and thereby acquire the cloak of authority.

3456789

*Maxular*, Steven Skaggs (2018)

The mark demands to be looked at; the word demands to be read. These two modes — looking and reading — are in such constant tension that it is impossible to concentrate at the same time on how words *look* and what words *say*. To establish the transformation to reading, two conditions must be met. First we have to know the notational code — the language itself. The clearest font in the world doesn't help us read Spanish if we don't understand the code that is the Spanish language. The second condition is that the notational code must be displayed in a clear way, obeying certain rules stipulated by a graphical tradition called orthography.

The meaning impulse is so strong, the authority of the printed word so great, that to check letter spacing an old typographers' trick is to turn a line of type upside down. Inverting the type hinders reading enough that our eyes may return to looking mode.

*Uppercut Angle* by Joachim Müller-Lancé (2011)

Speaking of Aretha Franklin, Dionne Warwick once said, "When Aretha reaches for a note to express a feeling, we call it squalling." Squalling is the reach, the gesture toward, the striving. It allows a moment to hear and feel the purity of emotion that lies behind, or underneath, the notes that are sung. Sometimes letter forms allow a kind of squalling, reveal the striving in the moment of their being made. In the same way that Aretha's audience feels the emotional tension in the squalled vocalization, a tension that will finally be released as the note is reached and the words are sung, written letters can move expressively toward final resolution. Just as squalling is not the note but the movement toward the note, writing and other graphical signs sometimes reveal the reaching itself. Such a gesture reflects, but transcends, the sense of struggle in the making, becoming pure expression. In the hands of an artist the mastery of that struggle, due to experience, practice, and skill, gives us a sense of rectitude, of just-rightness, a final resolution in both feeling and form. The best gospel, the best dancers, the best athletes, the best calligraphy, the best drawings, the best typefaces — they all reach this level of righteous flow, an inevitability that unites form, feeling, and purpose in an efficient and graceful whole.

 Edgy? Edgy? Edgy.

con ast &alittlebitofbufferspace?

In typography, clarity is a function of three factors: contrast, buffer space, and orthography.

The considerations of contrast and buffer space return us to form and perception. We have to see

edges to see a shape, and we have to be able to set off a letter's shape from other visual objects in the

environment that might hide it or make it difficult to perceive ...

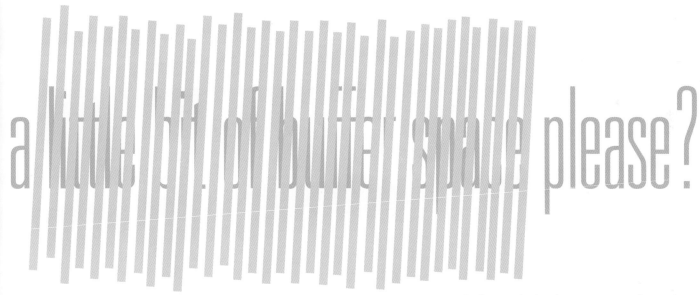

a little bit of buffer space please?

... Orthography is a bit more complicated:

Whereas looking enjoys novelty, orthography requires convention.

# Form & Legib

Adrian Frutiger's *Univers* is so legible because each glyph

approaches the form-norm of all familiar typefaces.

But orthography is more than the form of the letters. Orthography literally means "correct writing."

Orthography has to do with the way we string the letters together. In the West, we place them next to

each other from left to right on a horizontal line; we start sentences with capital letters, put a little more

space between words than between letters, and we spell words in a consistent way.  We do all of this so

that we can defeat the tendency to look at letters, and help the ability to read the meaning of the words.

If a painter had chosen to place a human head
On a horse's neck, covered a mixing of limbs,
Everywhere, with multi-coloured plumage, so
That what was a lovely woman, at the top,
Ended repulsively in the tail of an ugly fish:
Asked to a viewing, could you not laugh, my friends?
Believe me, dear Pisos, a book would be exactly like such
A picture, should it on a random whim be so conceived
That neither its head nor foot relate or correspond
To a unified form. But, you say, 'Painters and poets
Have always had equal privilege to try anything.'
True enough: I claim that license, and grant it in turn:
But not to the degree that tame and savage should mate,
Or serpents couple with birds, or lambs with tigers.
Pompous introductions and grand encomia often
Have appended one or two purple verses that
Make a great show, as in the grove and altar of Diana
Or of a current making its way through pleasant fields

Orthography tilts the odds toward reading and away from looking. When we read a conventional text, the words come forward in our consciousness while the form of the glyphs, the symbols that convey the language, fade into our subconscious.

*If a painter had chosen*

If we want a reader to become a viewer, a looker,

*On a horse's neck, cove*

to regain a sense of the graphic, to introduce a measure of squalling,

*Everywhere, with mult*

we have to place the text into unfamiliar conditions.

*That what was a lovely*

We feel the shift when we change the size or color ...

*Ended repulsively in th*

Humano capiti ceruicem pictor equinam
ingec si uelit et uarias inducere plumas
ndique collatis membris, ut turpiter atrum
esinat in piscem mulier formosa superne,
pectatum admissi, risum teneatis, amici?
redite, Pisones, isti tabulae fore librum
ersimilem, cuius, uelut aegri somnia, uanae
ngentur species, ut nec pes nec caput uni
eddatur formae. Pictoribus atque poetis   or when we see a foreign tongue …
uidlibet audendi semper fuit aequa potestas.
cimus, et hanc ueniam petimusque damusque uicissim,
ed non ut placidis coeant immitia, non ut
erpentes auibus geminentur, tigribus agni.
nceptis grauibus plerumque et magna professis
urpureus, late qui splendeat, unus et alter
dsuitur pannus, cum lucus et ara Dianae
t properantis aquae per amoenos ambitus agros
ut flumen Rhenum aut pluuius describitur arcus;
ed nunc non erat his locus. Et fortasse cupressum
cis simulare; quid hoc, si fractis enatat exspes
auibus, aere dato qui pingitur? Amphora coepit
nstitui; currente rota cur urceus exit?

had chosen to place a human head
's neck, covered a mixing of limbs,
, with multi-coloured plumage, so
was a lovely woman, at the top,
lsively in the tail of an ugly fish:
viewing, could you not laugh, my friends?
 dear Pisos, a book would be exactly like such
hould it on a random whim be so conceived
r its head nor foot relate or correspond or text placed unusually on a page …
l form. But, you say, 'Painters and poets
s had equal privilege to try anything.'
h: I claim that license, and grant it in turn:
he degree that tame and savage should mate,
s couple with birds, or lambs with tigers.
ntroductions and grand encomia often
ded one or two purple verses that
at show, as in the grove and altar of Diana
rent making its way through pleasant fields,
r Rhine, or the rainbow described.
ere was no room for these: perhaps, too,
ow to draw a cypress: but what is that
ose, if he, who is painted for given price,

or in orientations that are unconventional …

o capiti ceruicem pictor equinam
i uelit et uarias inducere plumas
collatis membris, ut turpiter atrum
n piscem mulier formosa superne,
m admissi, risum teneatis, amici?
Pisones, isti tabulae fore librum
em, cuius, uelut aegri somnia, uanae
r species, ut nec pes nec caput uni
formae. Pictoribus atque poetis
t audendi semper fuit aequa potestas.
et hanc ueniam petimusque damusque uicissim,
ut placidis coeant immitia, non ut
s auibus geminentur, tigribus agni.
grauibus plerumque et magna professis
us, late qui splendeat, unus et alter
pannus, cum lucus et ara Dianae
rantis aquae per amoenos ambitus agros
en Rhenum aut pluuius describitur arcus;
c non erat his locus. Et fortasse cupressum
ilare; quid hoc, si fractis enatat exspes
aere dato qui pingitur? Amphora coepit
currente rota cur urceus exit?

...RAPHY.

or anywhere the familiar rules of orthography are drastically violated ...

cato. Laqu

and especially when the the marking is obvious

Pulvini di

and carries forward the sense of the gestural flow,

lanugine t

cato. Laqu

an effect still seen in vestigial form in many fonts, especially those

Pulvini di

that hew close to the details of calligraphy, such as Bruce Rogers's *Centaur*.

lanugine t

In contrast, it is through those highly

**un**orthographic cases, through squalls (and scrawls),

that we are reminded that we readers are also

lookers, and we begin to regain, within words, the

song of expression, even as the verbal is lost.

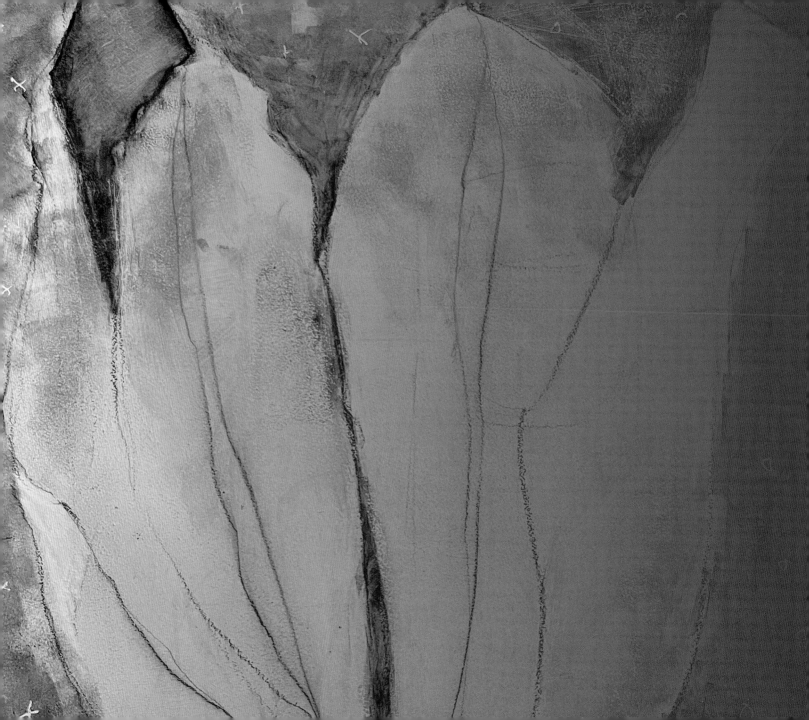

8

# Ambiguity and interplay

The mixed region where mark, image, and word combine

Sometimes, the mixture of image, mark, and word is so complete that the result is ambiguous. Is it a word or a picture? An abstract mark or an image of some subject? Or occasionally a mix of all three, as in this logo for Tymbal House Press.

In other cases, individual elements may clearly occupy different positions on the gamut,

but they are brought together compositionally to share the same space. Susan M. Hagan

uses the felicitous term "Inter-play" in referring to these combinatorial modes, especially

when they involve the mixing of words and images. When we realize that interplay includes

not only word and image but also marking, we are awakened to the diversity of expression

that is happening in every display of visual communication. Image and word (even strange

writing in some mysterious notational code) may overlap …

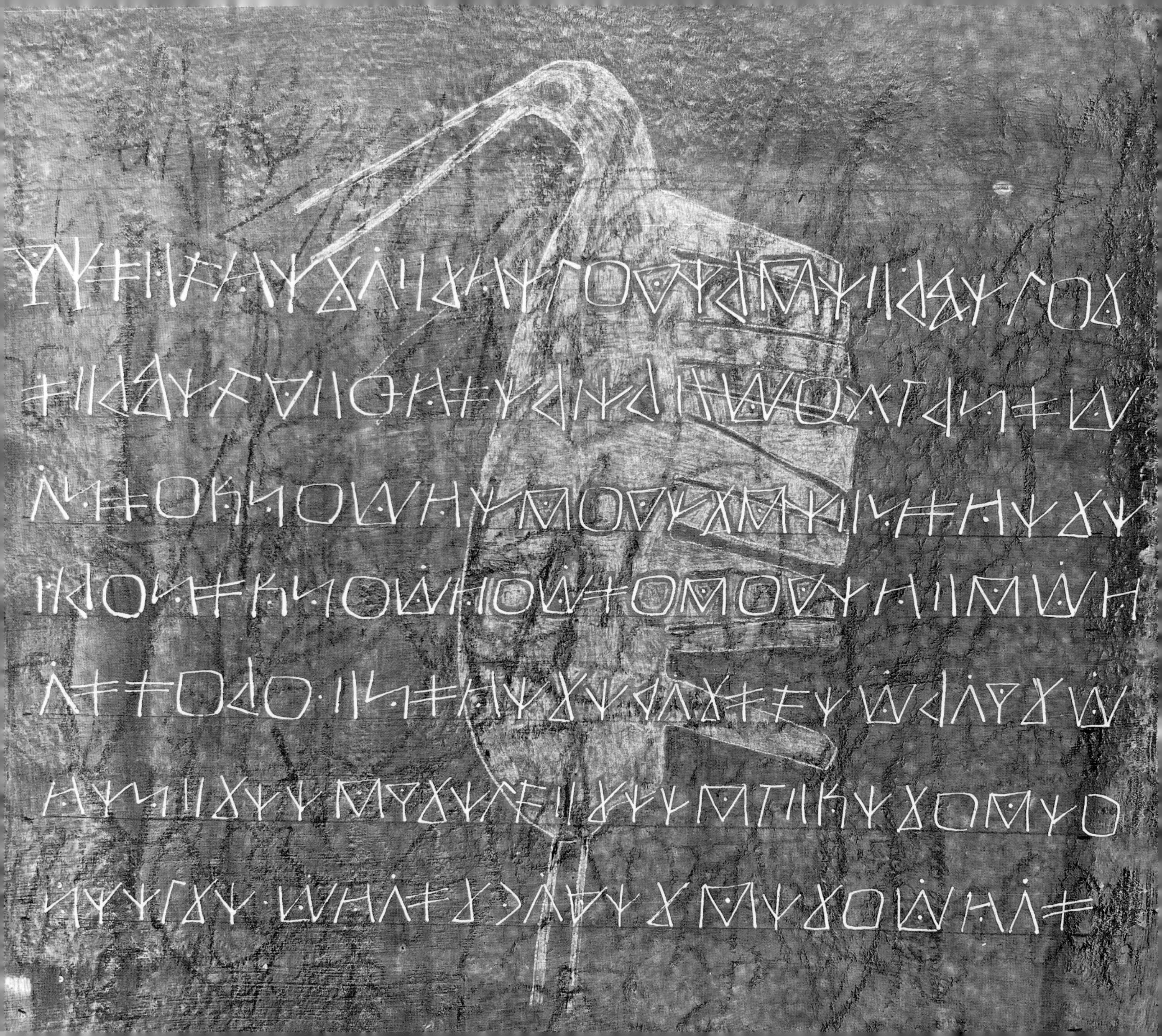

... but even in a drawing of a single subject, marking and image may interplay in a delicate

conversation. In this loosely rendered figure of a phoenix, two kinds of mark-making

combine: the more carefully drafted profile plays counterpoint to the exuberant gestures

in the drafting of the wing and tail. The artist, Laurie Doctor, gives us in equal measure

the outline shape of the bird's head and forewings, defining part of the image of the bird,

but also the energy that comes from the mystical bird as it rises, energy that is conveyed

through the vigorous expression of the gestural marking that completes the figure.

Indeterminate

Compounded

Fused

The ambiguous middle part of the gamut, then, suggests three kinds of situations. One is the ambiguity of a visual entity where you cannot be sure if it is an image, a mark, or a word. We say that its gamut mode is simply indeterminate. The two other situations involve kinds of interplay: visual entities occupy different gamut modes, but end up sharing the same compositional space. In the first kind of interplay, the separate entities are distinctly word, or mark, or image, but they overlap to make a compounded cluster in the visual composition; while in the second kind, exemplified by the painting of the phoenix, two gamut modes completely mix together to make a larger word or image (but never to make a larger mark). These "fused" cases are quite rare. Look around: see if you can find examples of fused ambiguous gamut modes. (Hint: It's what happens in a young child's coloring book before they learn to neatly stay within the lines!)

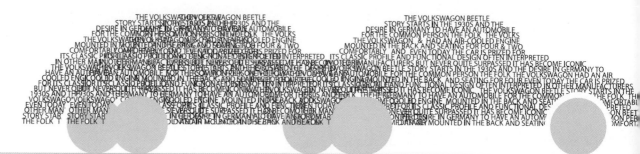

Fused

Venus rising over the
buttes in the east

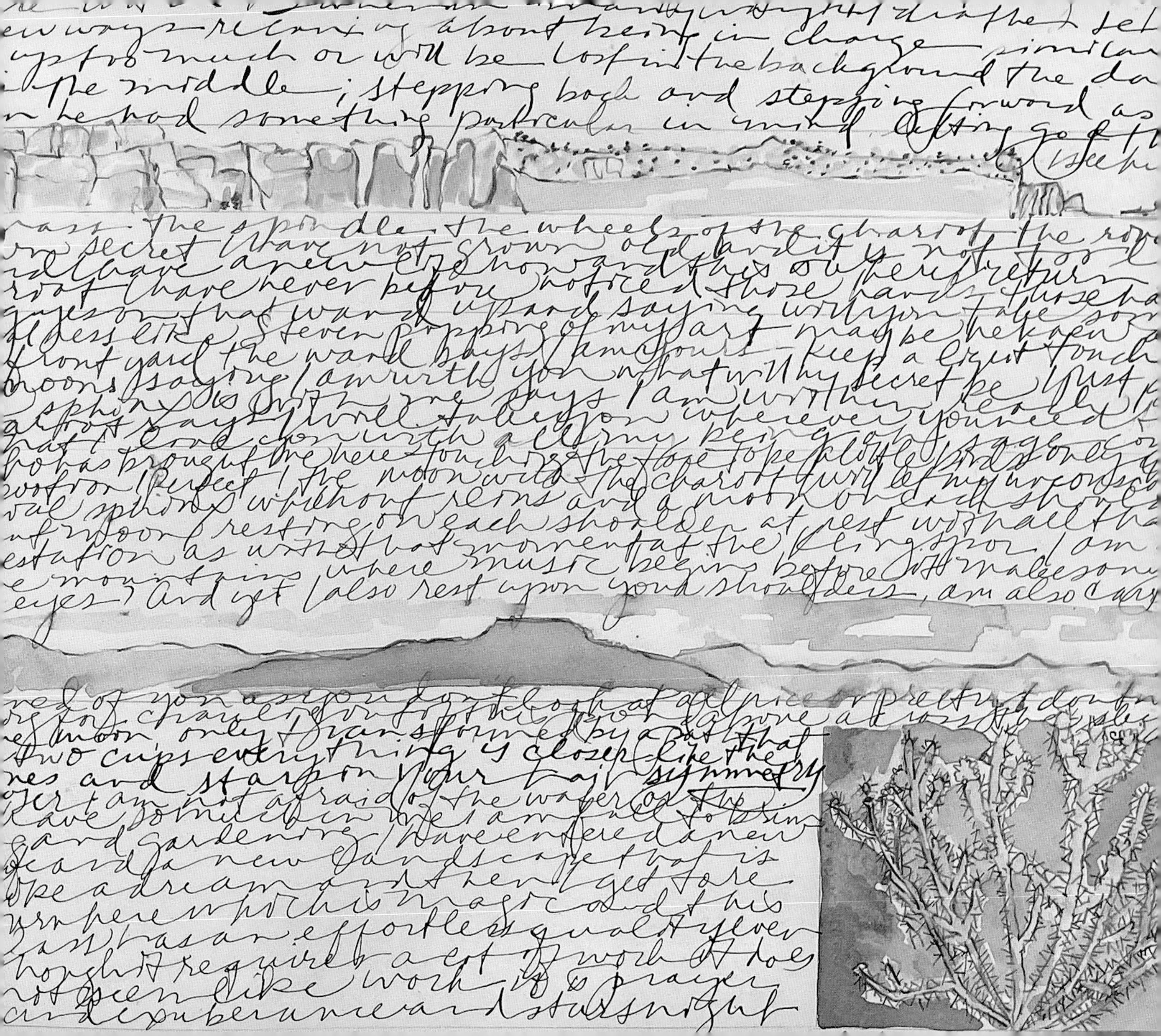
up too much or will be lost in the background the
the middle ; stepping back and stepping forward as
he had something particular in mind. letting go of th
eyes? And yet I also rest upon your shoulders, am also carry
two cups everything is closer like the
symmetry
nes and stars on your tray
I am not afraid of the water of the
and gardening I have entered a new
and a new landscape that is
has an effortless quality even
though it requires a lot of work it does
not seem like work it is prayer

In the end, it is not so important to be able to "correctly" identify the various ambiguities and

interplays as it is to be aware of them and acknowledge what vast resources for experimentation

we have in the visual arts. Various degrees of freedom in gesture, from the rapidly written to the

carefully constructed, can be combined to produce visual tension. For instance, placing a rigid,

inorganic digital element within or next to an organic gesture enhances the emotional contrast of

each. The point is that artists and designers have an enormous playground of possibilities to explore,

and using the gamut as a creative gaming tool can be a fine way of being present to the options.

ed. The hieroglyph of the
flamingo is for all thi
red: anger blood desert
rock pomegranate ro
sen green stones turquoise
malachite stars and gre
green that lets grow green green as a li
reed plant life light star death night des
rebirth halcyone lunch buy delicious coo
shade of green a fine unusual shade of gre
in life it is important to know how to do some
with with wit and flourish and style for som
else and do it fast—like pulling a sligh

These kinds of combination are nearly endless in their variety. But it is important to notice that they are made possible because we have learned, both through visual perception and through cultural practice, to treat visual objects that share boundaries such as page edges or picture frames not as separate objects but as a single message. The framing of elements within a page, or by the page itself, provides subcompositions within the larger message. The larger message is a display. The display's bounding by frames and edges informs us, the viewers, that we are being messaged, that we are receiving a signal, a set of communicative signs. Just as a plain white wall both highlights and reverences the work in an art exhibition, so the edges of a page and the limits of a screen announce that something is being shown to us. Edges tell us something is being displayed, meant for us to see, to understand. Edges not only define form, they also define message units.

9
Parting thoughts
mark / word — the primary tension

As suggested several times in this essay, nowhere within the visual gamut is tension so

deeply felt as in the hazy margin between mark and word. It is a kind of fault line between

two enormous tectonic plates: the world of sensual movement on one hand and the world

of reflection, thought, and language on the other. One is body, one is mind. One visually

dominant, one verbally dominant. Our culture tries to separate these two forces as much as

possible: dance and art departments on one side of campus, literature and creative writing

departments on the other side. But there is something we do every day that is precisely the

exploration of that forbidden fissure: the writing of words by hand.

Whether grocery list or love letter, the act of handwriting

brings mark-making squarely up against words. Looking

and reading collide. There is an art form whose subject

is precisely the exploration of that mark/word collision:

the art of calligraphy. Mention that word, and what

probably come to mind are cute sayings posted over the

coffee pot or crib: unflappably *nice*. As in trivial. Yet the

art is trivialized not because it is innately superficial, but

because it is innately discomforting. It's an inherently

transgressive art form. It transgresses by taking aim at

the visual/verbal fault line. We may think of calligraphy as

making pretty letters, but beyond the surface aesthetics

and the historicism, it is capable of so much more.

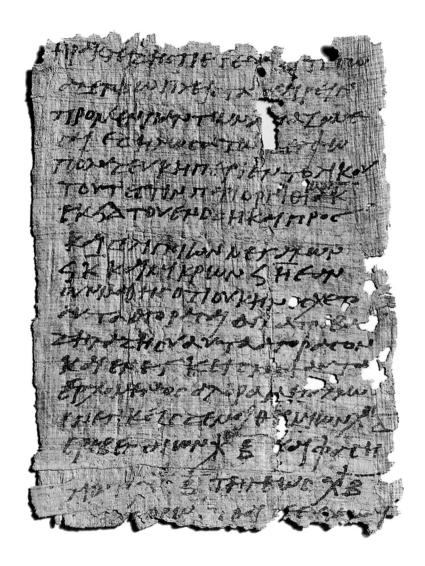

In Asia, where calligraphy is respected much more highly, it has long been accepted that precisely this ability to stir together the duality of conceptive language and haptic gesture, mind and body, presents the potential for works of formidable force. In Western calligraphic art, this power is most successfully found not in the works that have, as their purpose, the technical display of traditional lettering skill, but rather in the work of calligraphers who improvisationally walk the thin tightrope of legibility/illegibility.

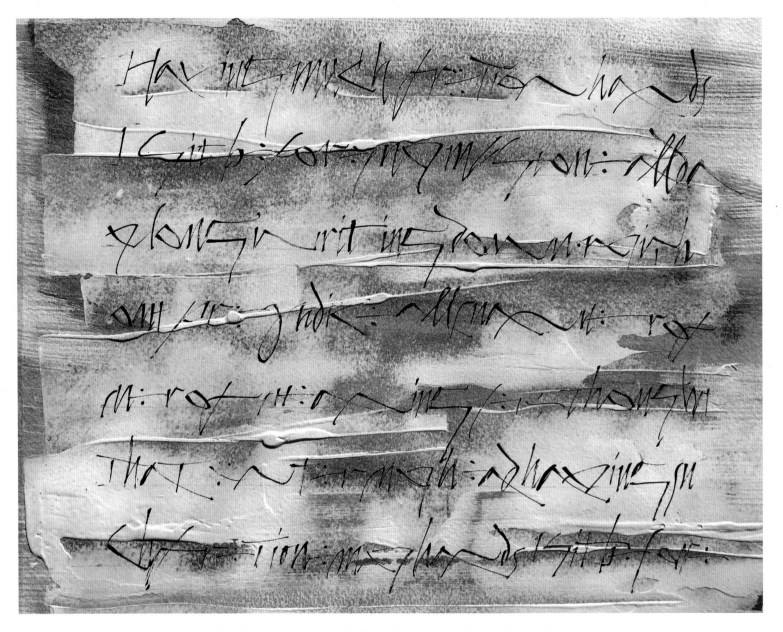

Such works invite the viewer to enjoy the feeling of the gesture first, only opening themselves to

language after the expenditure of time and effort, reversing the conventional role of the written word.

A palimpsest is a surface that has been written upon and then overwritten many times, leaving the under-writings partially visible. Assuming they are still legible, the writings reveal layers of verbal content, with all the possibilities for irony that a seemingly random collection of remarks affords. But the writing's forms, too, with their various families of gestures, may also belong to different visual worlds, and these combine like instruments in an orchestra of pulsing movement. Harmonious or discordant, emotionally effusive or formally remote, the form of language has its own song to sing. Perhaps that sense of the infinitude of personal emotion is why our culture's move from the penned and handwritten to the typed and texted, from the freehand drawing to the clip art emoticon, from stroking the pen to striking the keys, carries for some us a sense of loss.

element of logic. Here is a door and beyond here

OVETHEWAYSOMETHINGCO

For the shift from calligraphic gestures made by hand to the rational, stylized lines of typography is more

MESESSENTIALTOATOMATOT

than a "perfecting" of form. In the process, even though the basic flow of the strokes is retained in the

ASALTISAJAROFCRYSTALFR

typographic glyph, the sense of touch of the individual writer is lost, and with it, the material contact and

ARATEDFROMTHEOCEANE

immediacy that marking of any kind implies. We lose the sense that someone, writing in a particular place,

HEAVACADOSEPARATIONPE

at a particular pace, and in a specific mood, made the thing we see and hold. We lose the improvisations

IOFINALSEPARATIONTHESA

of momentary variations, the accidents caused by vagaries of surface, and most of all the *ductus*, that

JRNSTOTHEGROUNDANDW

pulsing breath of the sequence of strokes as the visual word becomes materially embodied through time.

TOTHESEAILOVETHEWAYSO

What is gained is a sense of permanence and authority, of absolute legibility and clarity of language.

ECOMESESSENTIALTOTAS

ecia formata, & cum el divi

demisse de ale, tegeua le

nua Hera, & cum divini e

vano delectamente jucur

el divini Olore trale delica

Tegeua le parte denudate

er cum el divino rostro obscurantise

negli amorosi amplexi

voluptici oblectamente jucundissimi

o. Laquale commodamen

Pulvini di panno doro

lanugine tomentati cum

vini di panno doro exqui

Et ella induta de vista Nympha

And with that authority and rationalization of the letter form, the perfect geometry of the legible sans serif typeface — gesture all but extinguished, the body ignored, the instant's movement abandoned to the settled fixed shape — language reassumes ascendancy, the mind regains control over the dangerous whims of the body, the eyes give way to the voice and to thought itself. Yet, in the implied vocalizations of that visual language, seemingly speaking directly to our minds with the authority of history, lurk the vestigial remnants of that primal movement of the hand, the kind of gesture that only humans make, the same kind of gesture that was once made by a Roman letter writer, an Egyptian scribe, all the way back to the first marks used as signs.

**Marks, the hidden factor, still lurking silently, and driving the form from within.**

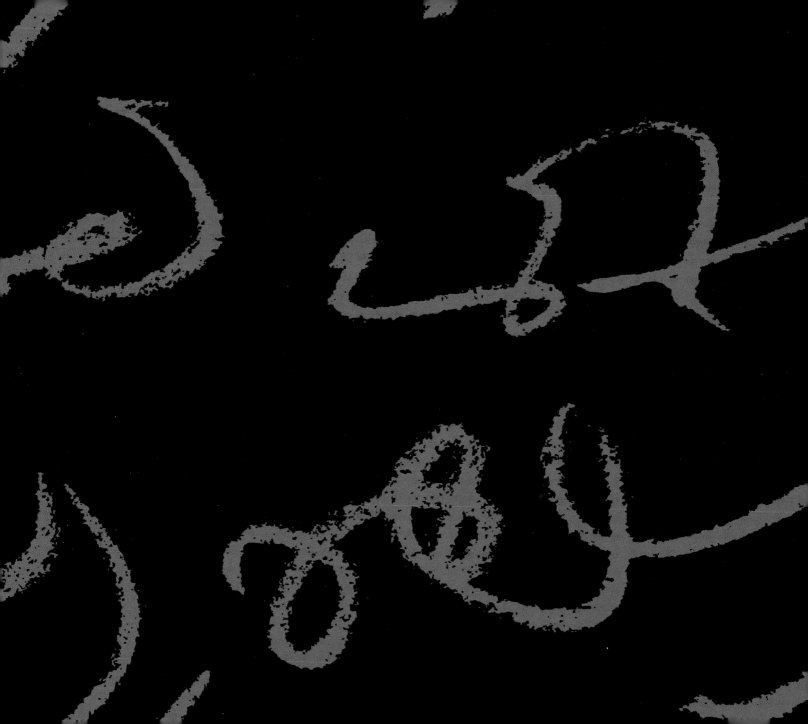

## References and notes

(listed in sequence by page number)

**ix.** Daniel Mendelowitz, *Drawing* (New York: Holt, Rinehart and Winston, 1967).

**ix.** Viktor Lowenfeld, *Creative and Mental Growth* (New York: Collier Macmillan, 1975).

**ix.** Rudolf Arnheim, *Visual Thinking* (Berkeley: University of California Press, 1969).

**ix.** Timothy Ingold, *Lines, a Brief History* (London: Routledge, 2007).

**x.** Marshall McLuhan and Quentin Fiore, *The Medium Is the Massage* (New York: Bantam Books, 1967).

**x.** George Nelson, *How to See* (New York: Little, Brown, 1977).

**x.** John Berger, *Ways of Seeing* (London: Penguin Classics, 2008).

**x.** April Greiman, *Hybrid Imagery* (New York: Watson-Guptill, 1990).

**x.** Bruce Mau, *Massive Change* (London: Phaidon, 2004).

**x.** Alan Fletcher, *The Art of Looking Sideways* (London: Phaidon, 2001).

**x.** Margaret Wise Brown, *Goodnight Moon* (New York: Harper, 1947).

**x.** Theodor Seuss Geisel, *Horton Hears a Who* (New York: Random House, 1954).

**x.** Maurice Sendak, *Where the Wild Things Are* (New York: Harper Collins, 1963).

**3.** "There is no visual entity without an edge." Although gestalt continuation and closure can permit us to *sense* an edge without a physical presence, even an illusory edge is an edge.

**25.** The field that studies signs and how they generate meaning is called semiotics.

**48–49.** Blackletter and Lombardic are considered different historic scripts because the manner in which they were written was distinctly different from humanistic, roman forms. Lombardic uses drawn outlines and blackletter does away with curves. By the time they are translated into drawn typographic characters, such arcane distinctions fall away.

**76.** For those interested in a deeper dive into semiotics, the visual gamut is inspired by Charles Sanders Peirce's notion of the three different ways a sign can stand for its referent: iconically (by likeness), indexically (by environmental contact), and symbolically (by consensual arbitrary connection). Technical discussion of the gamut and its extension into formal abstraction may be found in my *FireSigns* (Cambridge, MA: MIT Press, 2017) and "The Visual Gamut and Syntactic Abstraction," *Semiotica*, no. 244 (2022): 1–25.

**88.** Gerrit Noordzij, *The Stroke: Theory of Writing* (New York: Princeton Architectural Press, 2005).

**118.** *Aretha Franklin: The Queen of Soul,* screenplay by Nelson George, ed. Jody Sheff (A*Vision Entertainment, 1988).

**124–128.** The text on these pages is from Horace, *Ars poetica* (c. 18 BCE).

**136–137.** Laurie Doctor writing using her "Corridor" alphabet (2022).

**140.** Susan M. Hagan, *The Space between Look and Read: Designing Complementary Meaning* (Cambridge, MA: MIT Press, 2023). Hagan investigates the interaction of text and image to a remarkable degree, defining four types of interplay, using cohesive strategies including melding, blending, juxtaposition, and masking. At least two of these strategies, melding (fusing) and juxtaposition, are found in mark-image interplays.

**150.** Laurie Doctor's handwritten text is a fragment from Susan Brind Morrow's *The Names of Things: Life, A Passage in the Egyptian Desert* (New York: Riverhead Books, 1997).

**159–161.** Even if you know German, reading these takes time.

**164.** Laurie Doctor's handwritten text fragment is from Pablo Neruda's "Ode to Salt." It is written in an adaptation of Moon script, a notational code for the blind developed by William Moon in the 1840s.

This book is dedicated to my teachers, especially

Robert J. Doherty, who taught us to think,

Daniel Boyarski, who taught us to feel

John Pai, who taught us that Nature is the best teacher

and Hermann Zapf, who taught us "We are all brothers and sisters in this art"

and to my students

who taught me more than I taught them.

Special thanks to Laurie Doctor for access to *The Laurie Doctor Sketchbooks*.
More of Laurie's work can be found at www.lauriedoctor.com.

Book design by Steven Skaggs

Illustration credits